LIFE CYCLE OF A...

Pumpkin

Calabaza

Revised and Updated

Ron Fridell
and
Patricia Walsh

Heinemann Library
Chicago, Illinois

Edited by Adrian Vigliano, Harriet Milles, and Diyan Leake
Designed by Kimberly R. Miracle and Tony Miracle
Original illustrations ©Capstone Global Library Limited
2001, 2009
Illustrated by David Westerfield
Picture research by Tracy Cummins and Heather Mauldin
Originated by Chroma Graphics (Overseas) Pte. Ltd.
Printed in China

15 14
10 9 8 7

New edition ISBNs: 978 1 4329 2527 7 (hardcover)
978 1 4329 2544 4 (paperback)

**The Library of Congress has cataloged the first edition
as follows:**
Fridell, Ron.
Life cycle of a pumpkin / by Ron Fridell, Patricia Walsh.
p. cm.
Includes bibliographical references (p.) and index.
ISBN 1-58810-093-6 ISBN 978-1-58810-093-1 (lib. Bdg.)
1.Pumpkin—Life cycles—Juvenile literature. [1.
Pumpkin.]
I.Title: Pumpkin. II. Walsh., Patricia, 1951- III. Title
SB347 .F75 2001
635'.62—dc21

00-011234

Acknowledgments
The author and publishers are grateful to the following for
permission to reproduce copyright material: Getty Images
p. **27** (©Andy Sacks); iStockphoto pp. **11** (©gmnicholas), **14**,
29 top left (©grapegeek), **17** (©GomezDavid); ©Dwight Kuhn
pp. **7, 8, 9, 19, 20, 28 top right**; Photolibrary pp. **12, 15, 28
bottom** (©Index Stock Imagery), **10** (©Index Stock Imagery/
Samuel Taylor), **13** (©Gimmi Gimmi), **16, 29 top right**
(©Brand X Pictures), **21** (©Stockbyte), **26** (©FoodCollection);
Shutterstock pp. **4** (©Marilyn Volan), **5** (©A.L. Spangler), **6**,
28 top left (©Jaroslaw Grudzinski), **18** (©Eric Litton), **22**,
29 bottom (©Chris LeBoutillier), **23** (©Elena Elisseeva), **24**
(©TheSupe87), **25** (©Monkey Business Images).

Cover photograph of a pumpkin reproduced with permission
of Jupiter Images (©Gary Moss).

Every effort has been made to contact copyright holders of
any material reproduced in this book. Any omissions will
be rectified in subsequent printings if notice is given to the
publisher.

We would like to thank Michael Bright for his invaluable help
in the preparation of this book.

Contents

What Is a Pumpkin? 4

Seed 6

Seedling 8

Vine 10

Flower 12

Pollination 14

Growing and Ripening 16

Problems for Pumpkins 18

Harvest 20

After the Harvest 22

Next Year's Pumpkins 26

Life Cycle 28

Fact File 30

Glossary 31

More Books to Read 32

Index 32

Some words are shown in bold, **like this**. You can find out what they mean by looking in the glossary.

What Is a Pumpkin?

Pumpkins can be orange, white, yellow, or red.

2 A pumpkin is a fruit. It grows on a **vine** like other kinds of **squash**. Pumpkins can be bumpy or smooth, large or small, and long or round.

Seed	1 week	2 weeks	10 weeks

2 Pumpkins have hard skins with deep lines that go from top to bottom.

Each year there is a new **crop** of pumpkins.

11 weeks

14 weeks

16 weeks

Seed

Each pumpkin has lots of seeds inside it.

Pumpkins begin as **seeds**. The seeds have an oval shape. A tiny plant is curled up inside each seed.

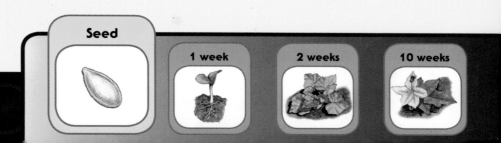

Seed

1 week

2 weeks

10 weeks

The seed is planted in warm, damp soil. In about ten days, a root grows down into the soil. The root takes in water and food for the plant. Tiny leaves push up into the sunlight.

Can you see the tiny leaf breaking out of the seed?

Seedling

The first two leaves pop through the soil. The tiny new plant is called a seedling. The leaves use sunlight, water, and air to make food for the new plant.

The first leaves to come out of the **seed** are called seed leaves.

Seed

1 week

2 weeks

10 weeks

The true leaves grow big very quickly.

Then the true leaves appear. They are jagged and prickly. The job of the seed leaves is done. They **wither** and fall off.

11 weeks

14 weeks

16 weeks

Vine

Fully grown pumpkin leaves can be bigger than a person's head!

The pumpkin plant grows more leaves. The plant grows quickly and soon becomes a **vine**. The vine twists and creeps along the ground.

Seed

1 week

2 weeks

10 weeks

Vine tendrils can twist around fences or sticks.

The vine sends out thin **tendrils**. They grab and curl around other vines. The tendrils support the vine as it grows longer and longer.

11 weeks

14 weeks

16 weeks

Flower

The small ball at the base of the female flower is a new pumpkin waiting to grow.

The pumpkin **vine blooms** with many yellow flowers. Some of these are female flowers. Female flowers sit on small, fuzzy green balls.

Seed · 1 week · 2 weeks · 10 weeks

It takes a male and a female flower to make a pumpkin.

Other flowers are male flowers. They grow on long stems. The flowers have a yellow powder inside, called **pollen**.

11 weeks

14 weeks

16 weeks

Pollination

A bee visits the male flowers. The pollen sticks to the bee's body and legs.

It also takes bees to make pumpkins. The **pollen** rubs off on bees as they go in and out of the flowers. Bees move the pollen from male flowers to female flowers.

| Seed | 1 week | 2 weeks | 10 weeks |

The female flower dies as the pumpkin starts to grow.

The pollen reaches a female flower. Now the fuzzy green ball at the end of the flower begins to grow into a pumpkin.

11 weeks

14 weeks

16 weeks

Growing and Ripening

All summer the **vines**, **tendrils**, and leaves of the plant grow and tangle together. Underneath the big leaves are little pumpkins.

The pumpkins start to change color as they grow bigger.

Seed	1 week	2 weeks	10 weeks

The pumpkin's big leaves protect the pumpkin fruit.

The leaves are like big umbrellas. They keep the hot sunshine off the pumpkins. They help to keep the soil around the pumpkins from drying out.

11 weeks

14 weeks

16 weeks

Problems for Pumpkins

Growing pumpkins need just the right amount of water and sunshine. Too much rain **rots** the pumpkins. Too much sunshine **withers** the **vines**.

This pumpkin has started to rot.

Seed	1 week	2 weeks	10 weeks

Beetles can eat pumpkin flowers and damage them.

Beetles and other insects can hurt the growing pumpkins, too. Farmers cover the vines with nets, or spray the plants with **insecticides** to protect them.

11 weeks

14 weeks

16 weeks

Harvest

Pumpkin seeds can be good to eat when they are roasted.

The pumpkins grow bigger and bigger. Inside, the pumpkins form **seeds** and **pulp**. Outside, the pumpkins' color turns from green to orange.

| Seed | 1 week | 2 weeks | 10 weeks |

A big pumpkin can be very heavy to lift.

Then the **vines** turn brown. **Harvest** time has come. The farmer cuts the thick pumpkin stem from the vine.

11 weeks

14 weeks

16 weeks

After the Harvest

These pumpkins will be sold in stores and farmers' markets.

Four months ago there were only **seeds**. Now the farmer has **harvested** a wagon full of round, orange pumpkins.

| Seed | 1 week | 2 weeks | 10 weeks |

People like to cook pumpkins. They use the **pulp** to make pumpkin pies and soup. In some countries, pumpkins are used to feed farm animals.

Homemade pumpkin pie is a delicious treat!

11 weeks

14 weeks

16 weeks

After the Harvest

In late summer or the fall, some places hold fairs. Sometimes there is a competition to find who grew the biggest pumpkin.

This big pumpkin has won first place in a competition!

Seed

1 week

2 weeks

10 weeks

At Halloween, pumpkins can be carved to look like scary faces.

Many pumpkins are scooped out and carved for Halloween. People put candles inside the pumpkins to make them glow with an orange light.

11 weeks

14 weeks

16 weeks

Next Year's Pumpkins

Inside the pumpkin there are many **seeds**. Some seeds are roasted to be eaten as snacks. Other seeds are saved to be planted in the spring.

These seeds will grow into next year's pumpkins.

Seed	1 week	2 weeks	10 weeks

When the field is plowed, it is ready for planting seeds again in the spring.

After the pumpkins are picked and sold, the farmer **plows** the field. Old **vines** and unpicked pumpkins get mixed with the soil.

11 weeks

14 weeks

16 weeks

Life Cycle

Seed

Seedling

Vine and flowers

Pollination

Growing pumpkins

Harvest

Fact File

-  The biggest pumpkin on record was grown in Rhode Island in 2007. It weighed as much as a horse!

- The Irish were the first people to carve Halloween lights from vegetables.

- Different types of pumpkins have different names, such as Sugar Pie, Atlantic Giant, Baby Boo, and Cinderella.

- Pumpkins come from the same plant family as cucumbers, **squashes**, melons, and watermelons.

- A pumpkin **vine** might have flowers all summer, but each flower **blooms** for only one day.

Glossary

bloom when flowers open up

crop food grown in one season

harvest gathering of a crop

insecticide poison that kills insects

plow to turn over and mix up the soil

pollen grains of yellow powder that are released from male flowers

pulp soft, fleshy part of a fruit or vegetable

rot decay, spoil

seed part of a plant that can grow into a new plant

squash fruit like a pumpkin

tendril long, thin part of a plant stem that grabs and curls around things to help the plant climb or spread

vine plant with long, thin stems that grows along the ground, or climbs up things

wither dry up and shrink

More Books to Read

Ganeri, Anita. *How Living Things Grow: From Seed to Apple.* Chicago: Heinemann Library, 2006.

Schaefer, Lola. *Food Groups: Vegetables.* Chicago: Heinemann Library, 2007.

Index

bees 14
color 5, 20
fairs 24
flower 12–13, 14, 15
harvest 20–21, 22, 24, 29
lantern 25, 30
leaves 7, 8, 9, 10, 16, 17
pollination 14–15, 29

problems 18–19
seed 6–7, 20, 22, 26, 27, 28
seedling 8–9, 28
squash 4, 30
vine 4, 10–11, 12, 16, 18, 19, 21, 27, 28, 30